RESISTING
PROBABILITY

COLIN JAMES

© 2017 by Colin James

All Rights Reserved.

Set in Williams Caslon Text with LaTeX.

ISBN: 978-1-944697-50-1 (paperback)
ISBN: 978-1-944697-51-8 (ebook)
Library of Congress Control Number: 2017910609

Sagging Meniscus Press
saggingmeniscus.com

Acknowledgements

Some of these poems have appeared in the following magazines:

Cenacle, Outlaw Poetry, Boyslut, Anti-Heroin Chic, Damfino, Gaptoothed Madness, Concrete Wolf, Z-Composition Magazine, The Toucan, Hand Job Zine, The Prospect Review, Polluto, Kaleidotrope, and *Bad Nudes.*

For Jane

Contents

That Which Appropriates · *1*

The Envious are Grateful Lovers · *2*

Dead Feints or Spasms of Insurrection · *3*

Fagantown · *4*

Farmers Market of Organic Egos · *5*

The Suppressive Have Never Embraced Conformity · *6*

Fine Ideals · *7*

Measures Ex Post Facto · *8*

The Decline of Circuses, Sea World and Homosexual Metaphors · *9*

The Un-come-atable Panorama · *10*

Auteur · *11*

The Barely Presentable Refugee · *12*

A Summary of My Limitations · *13*

Guido the Unknown · *14*

As Joseph Adjusts his Charisma · *15*

The Second Most Sought After · *16*

Existing in the Space Provided · *17*

Drivers Wanted · *18*

The Evolution of the Gun Shot · *19*

Idols of the Cave · *20*

Idols of the Tribe · *21*

Idols of the Marketplace · *22*

Idols of the Theater · *23*

Dominatrix of the Boneyard · *24*

In Deference to the Rueful Night · *25*

Dave's Sobriquet Search for Sobriety · *26*

The Moral Ambiguities of a Tall Person · *27*

Traveling Through Time · *28*

The Posthumous Behind · *29*

Notifying Several Antagonists of Their Obligations · *30*

Conjugal Visits and the Rise in Absenteeism · *31*

The Home Invasion Enthusiast · *32*

The Abnormal Mind · *33*

Great Scott Humanized · *34*

The Class of 3000 · *35*

Expanding the Parameters of Romanticism · *36*

The Lascivious Labyrinths of Considerate Rivals · *37*

Establishing Then Severing All Communiques · *38*

The Posthumous Wretch · *39*

The Panic Part of the Procedure · *40*

A Disturbed Perspective · *41*

Red is the Color of My True Love's Horse · *42*

The Calming Disorder of Irrational Tendencies · *43*

The Conceptual, It's an Experience · *44*

Straight Swap · *45*

Gratification in the Archipelago · *46*

A Contract Existing to Encourage the Comparison of the Imparticular · *47*

Oh's Arm Wrestling Emporium · *48*

Impreciseness and Recessive Pronunciations · *49*

Micro-Managing by Jiminy · *50*

Relaxation in its Ethereal Aesthetic · *51*

Mentors of the Impervious · *52*

Resisting Probability · *53*

A Landscape's Long Memory · *54*

Malapropisms of the Mezzanine · *55*

Resisting
Probability

That Which Appropriates

It took up most of the kitchen
& a good portion of the hallway floor.
A queue had begun to form in the early hours
& now extended many blocks
ending at the Jordan's house under
the large oak with the cement reinforcement.
Young Sally was running the lemonade stand.
She was unable to answer the reporter's question
regarding frequency of use,
& quickly coalesced.
Her desperate ad-lib stalling for time.
"It's like the snack from hell!"

The Envious are Grateful Lovers

Negro auras are the most difficult to detect.
Many times I have stood beneath
the inquisitive shade of my umbrella
waiting for just the right light
to filter the monotheistic.
As it turns out you are not the one.
I suppose this means further deprivation
until our cluttered rooms burst
to reveal their golden hue.

Head Feints or Spasms of Insurrection

The signals were small fires
on top of hills and cairns.
We were but a band of desperadoes
unable to make our way
by following the lights.
The slime of death was everywhere.
There was little food left
& water not a negotiable commodity.
When the fires ceased
we knew we were close,
but grew increasingly skeptical
when our most dependable scout
returned with his appendage tied
into an indulgent eagle knot.
It would take twelve hours before
we could get the kinks out.

Pagantown

Occurring flotsam in the canal's
narrow channels are really
two bodies bumping heads.
A first fisherman would
compare them to floating tires,
wives warm in bed. His net
a wind-caught singing cloak.
A second fisherman would
complain of cold coffee
and ponder the greying flesh.
"The bodies should be saved
from the fish!" A passing
postman is asked to notify
the authoritative curve,
a framed graph in the town
square. The town's population
is reduced by two & graph's
curve softens its arc.
The fishermen appear somber.
They have just an hour before daylight,
& they must begin their work.

Farmers Market of Organic Egos

The blonde in plaid is leading me to her booth,
a sturdy door above four milk crates.
She stores her perishables on dry ice.
Is that the boyfriend looming?
Tall & wiry, suspiciously upbeat.
Bearded, he looks like a horny prophet.
Dirty fingernails from handling The Earth.
I like the look of her tomatoes.
They grow if you water them.
Adjacent booths and the selling of the same.
Must remember to purchase enough perennials.

The Suppressive Have Never Embraced Conformity

Uselessly losing weight
had become forbidden
as we paused
at the bench you
refer to as
your Mench,
& Clorox wiped
the iron parts while
watching the young bloods
become prophetic
in their way.

Nine Ideals

Follow the wall down to the sea,
landowners may defer in emergencies.
Ivy grows despite the salt air & deer.
Ignore the hard drink and philosophy,
pause a while on the smooth stone.
Many character flaws are cured here,
whines lost to the wind. Kneel carefully
as not to disturb the pragmatic
predisposed for the familiar.
The shakedown dance-like
factoring in a margin for error.
This dominance is synonymous
with cultural advantage,
& you were suddenly dressed differently.
The banana skins of sorrow
playing for time, an affectation
that would eventually fit in.
So innocently centered,
the sensual will repel
like a bull's-eye.

Pleasures Ex Post Facto

The neighbor's white elephant
has destroyed all the young trees
that are within his reach.
I was considering his poop for fertilizer
but my reasoning has regressed to the provincial.
The elephant has lost an eye & furtively
draws attention to it by dusting
the air around his small sky.
I visit and we talk in muted grunts.
Snorts can indicate an emphatic debate.
His circus abused & abandoned him.
Disfigurement reduced his desirability.
This winter will be difficult.
He informs me of his desire
to return home where god willing
he could look up some old mates.

The Decline of Circuses, Sea World and Homosexual Metaphors

The church bookstore bathroom
has a stone floor
& real white ceramic rails
hanging a fresh cloth hand towel.
Plenty to read
as I drop a deuce
slightly wind-torn
& wondering if my sounds echo
like the volunteer's acrimonious
soliloquies do.

The Un-come-atable Panorama

The portal to an alternative universe
has recently been identified
by a Peter Allman
of Ellesmere Port, Cheshire.
Mr. Allman was fortunate
to obtain several controversial photos
due to overcast conditions
on his cell phone before
the portal was no longer expressive.
He lists his hobbies as
train spotting, stamp collecting
& alternative universe enthusiast.
Memorabilia can be purchased
by contacting Mr. Allman at
a not particularly enigmatic
gypsy caravan in Anglesey, Wales.

Auteur

We all know one.
Herculean beard like a showgirl's nest,
his very large shadow until light intersects
coughing extemporaneous fits within
these aquamarine white willed walls.
Breakfast tent squats, stripped
the great man is up.
His partner shops in the market.
Bountiful baskets of olives, dates, grapes.
Today their lunch guest is a cat.
A telegram announcing apologies.
The Iranian prince incapacitated while water skiing.
Loves the script, but regrets..........

The Barely Presentable Refugee

To unobtrusively loiter is a gift.
Some don't have it, obviously, so
better to engage a pro.
Filling out paperwork clandestinely
hanging with those type of virtues,
garners a balanced distraction, a closet.
Your hireling waits dressed
in small clown shoes and beard.
Soon enough the ceiling is crowded
with demanding I need this nows.
Table settings precariously
hang down from above.
Some people are never so traditionally served.
They hover ever, ignored obsessively.

A Summary of My Limitations

I painted a small crowd,
people on plastic cutouts
details down to hair texture
became allusively representative.
Held off on some expressions
like staring in mid-thought.
Life size and transportable,
I placed them at various corners
near houses of copious civility.
They milled about, held
imaginary conversations, smoked.
Conceptual in their bathroom brakes
like vandals impersonal, aloof,
wary of destruction for its own sake.

Guido the Unknown

The men drank their absinthe and waited.
Outside the sound of climbing
like tending to the aspherical.
Someone was on the roof again.
Perhaps an early yard sale participant.
In thirty years of two biannual distractions,
only one neighbor committed halfheartedly.
A lone oak chair sat midway up his driveway.
A small threatening sign for a price tag
Keep Out! Two Hundred Dollars.

As Joseph Adjusts his Charisma

Sure there's contour
among the bodies in the bushes,
as there are notebooks on the flora.
It's the coughing that's unnerving
idolatry, haltering.
May as well be at the beach, staring.
I am just walking my dog, man.
The cars come around the corner fast
their high beams blind me momentarily.
I see nothing else on these cloudless nights,
other than these wanderings.
Someone threw you back
as I would an old T-shirt.
Your followers and
their flickering torches
extend like comparisons
over a series of small hills.
They are spaced out eventually
hidden in seamless rhythm.
Voices can do the same
without the patience.
How were we realistically
able to find a ride back into town?
It still bothers me to this day.
Before then, I had
never met the Druid
I couldn't bargain with.

The Second Most Sought After

The sanctuary's garden was virtual.
You sat in a stone chair and a holograph displayed.
Fifteen minutes absolute.
The rigidity of the stone was necessary
to keep your torso in movement.
Music was incidental Celine.
Peripherally, the waiting lines of escapists
were visible if you strained, which was not suggested.
You could see one of the eyes of each.
Eventually grayness framed the facade
and concentration payed off
in the form of pristine images.
Hobbit shacks and festering brooks.
A button could be pressed on the chair's crotch.
A drawer delivered tepid tap water.
Humming was allowed.
When the "ONE MINUTE TO NORMALITY" warning
sounded, it was best to prepare by twisting your head
from side to side and stretching arms and legs
in the opposite direction for which they were intended.
Celine's lovely euphony decreased to a barely audible whisper
and an escalator path caused the floor to move toward
a welcoming door. As soon as you consented you were replaced.

Existing in the Space Provided

The wood nymphs in my garden
are without merit.
They stole the light bulbs
from my shed.
The ones I was saving
for next Spring,
and carried them to
a moss covered arbor
deep in the woods.
They mistook
the warm lights
for enchantment.
I shall have to steal them back,
perhaps replace them with
something less than perfect.

Drivers Wanted

I am dining in a reasonably good restaurant.
I know this because I'm half way through the entrée
& eye contact has not yet been necessary.
Conversations murmur toward the ceilings.
Mother has been sorting without permission
my clothes by color & texture of cloth,
which makes it awkward when I try
to appear dashingly evasive like this.

The Evolution of the Gun Shot

First nothing,
then a fish slithered
onto dry land.
Soon after our lead guitarist
became ill
and we had to replace him
with someone who couldn't play.
Miraculously
we got booked on a world tour.
Now, after developing
a steady series of innovative aliases,
our first North American guitarist
is really starting to settle in.

Idols of the Cave

At the poetry reading
it became apparent
that the poet was not well.
He was an albino
with unhealthy-looking skin
and incredibly long
eyebrows and eyelids
that hung down over his face
like Spanish moss.
He read in a barely discernible whisper
that had us on the edge of our seats
trying to catch a word.
At the end of his reading he asked
if there were any questions.
A person near me stood up and said,
"You look like Andy Warhol's ghost!
How is Andy?"

Idols of the Tribe

I was awarded "The Most Unlikely
To Attend But Showed Up Anyway"
award at my high school reunion.
It was presented on a toilette roll
magic marker orange flowers,
green semblance of undigested
grass dripping backsides.
The presenter looked vaguely familiar.
That voice, Betsy something or other.
Very peppy, even now after much divorce.
The relevant embracing the irrelevant
with firm handshakes and sensible smiles.

Idols of the Marketplace

Left the embalmer's studio
and got a haircut as instructed
to temporarily relieve a cowlick.
Followed my yoga-pant-wearing therapist
up a long flight of stairs without complaint.
Sat in an imitation plastic chair
and confided in her questions.
Avoided the topic of her cat
with the two meanings.
Returned to work not particularly energized
since the dour image of conformity,
initiated by the eye contact-less
disrupted my rhythm of arrival.
Cleaned the computer screen thoroughly.
Responded to the Sygo Cooperation in Sweden,
assuring them the arrival of their polymers was imminent.
Stood over a rather foul-smelling urinal,
while contemplating a seemingly hastily drawn mural
which needlessly chewed on its theme,
the iconic face of Jesus.

Idols of the Theater

The voyeurs watched themselves
which was a bit awkward,
and we asked them to move on
as this was a public retreat.
The sea and land seemed
to attract every type of commoner
if you bother to account for spontaneity,
that candid right to sensibilities.
The food was tepid, crackers and flax.
Speeches occurred as soon as possible,
some skill set of primeval need
awakened by marginalized elocution.
Had to share the ride back
with a couple of biddies from Wrexham,
who complained all the way
about a driftwood sculpture that
was set afire near their tent.

Dominatrix of the Boneyard

You had to cut through
her backyard then a cemetery
to get to the convenience store,
unless you took the long way
crossing several intersections
sidewalks not of the hierarchical
indifferent, crowded, unextraordinary.
Her clothesline hung over two fences
besides a junked car
& an old deaf & blind dog.
We sat in the crab grass
watching her bras
set the wind direction
as they filled with air.
Stringed corsets hung low to the ground
touching each clothes pinned shoulder.
Red & black lace, white or pinkish.
Some lights from the small house
flickered as if tired or overburdened, went out
smouldered, then came back on again.

In Deference to the Rueful Night

Just stepped out of the office
to purchase a sandwich
from Ohare's Kosher Delicatessen
& was crossing the Curt
Schilling Memorial Bridge
when an unsuccessful jumper
clambered back up the side,
the river basin dry as denial.
She was about nineteen,
parents both relapsed alcoholics,
boyfriend neanderthal violative.
She consented to join me
for coffee and sandwiches. We sat
near an air conditioner and talked.
I got her a taxi home agreeing
to meet the next day, but never
saw her again. Double-checked all
the nostalgic skylines I could find.

Dave's Sobriquet Search for Sobriety

Fanatical Dave stood in line
at the dispensary. His
sunglasses incomplete aviators,
one lens partially missing
creating a prophetic effect.
The whole back of his leather jacket
entrusted to a green Chinese dragon
asleep on a black frozen lake.
He shared a cigarette
with a very young-looking girl
he may have fucked in another life.
Filled his lungs with smoke,
exhaled a stalactite-like salivary
breath of apathetic need.

The Moral Ambiguities of a Tall Person

An empty room.
The cave-like space
beneath the sink is covered
by a ludicrously dirty cloth.
A fold-up chair and tiny table
have been stored here.
When these are moved
to the center of the room
things don't improve.
At least there was hope before,
now there is only sadness.

Traveling Through Time

Passive histrionics
levitating beneath a rock.
Servitude's meandering cracks,
where did I put that's.
Forever and ever or
a horizon of stoics.
Impractically industrious.
I don't recall witnessing a fellow spirit
materialize without a comma
within the here is.

The Posthumous Behind

Objectified, she walks.
My head is in my hands
A long way from useful participation,
having to send messages
that have no effect other
than arriving without consequence.
Ours is a shared sulk
through buildings of high art,
too high by society's subtle standards.
I'm buying lunch for the whole room
after confirming it is conventionally empty.
Her steps by now sound very far away.
The last part of her to leave the room
stays with me as if it never left.

Notifying Several Antagonists of Their Obligations

I left the bathroom door
open for the hell hound.
If I don't, I can hear his
raspy asthmatic breathing
as pools of his thick
ABBA-fixated drool forms
under the doors cusp.
He sits now quite comfortably,
I on the other hand struggle
with the idea being not the reason
for the photograph he has just taken
while his preoccupation
with my formal posture wilts.

Conjugal Visits and the Rise in Absenteeism

Fried bread tied to a leather string
pings like a fetishist's wind chime.
It rattles all the lazy nerves,
awakens the spectacle of optimism.
Even with these adequate supplies
adjusted for parables,
confirmation cannot be.
Common sense says follow the river.
We attention-seekers crave the isolation,
yet somehow are able to overcompensate
& remain stoically unaware of the difference.

The Home Invasion Enthusiast

A cordon of papers prevents
the typical short-legged hop entrance.
Instead, a bent-over attitude prevails.
Ungrateful sighs are administered
during this telepathy of tact.
Spotless calm, as in nearly jammed.
Please direct me to the master bedroom,
I have a collection of curios to administer.
Your bedside table machine exemplifies a love-maker's
    whimsy.
See, everywhere an army of offspring trackers
or just smelly socks.
Needlessly, so much more of everything.

The Abnormal Mind

There is not enough time
to lift the heavy stone,
roll it down the steep hill,
wait with trepidation
as it balances uneven terrain,
observe its catastrophic power
smashing into the stranger's car,
and make it back home in time
to watch the TV version.

Great Scott Humanized

Admittedly, a landscape of sequined arses.
These tremors in drag as inconsiderate
as any four AM ritual.
Those dam pyres are still smoldering
and the postman's bike
is at the garden gate,
as the sun coughs itself
into the morning sky.

The Class of 3000

A clothesline made of thongs
and reusable coffee filters.
The debris of old knights
curled up in fingerless gloves.
In this addiction-only benediction,
I should have fucked you
up against that cement girder
except my behavior would not.
At least that's my estimate,
as I was left-handedly preoccupied
and formulating a thrill.

Expanding the Parameters of Romanticism

A certain celebrity's vagina is rumored
to smell like cataleptic mushrooms
from the northern regions of France,
slightly seasoned with garlic then
cooked in extra virgin olive oil.
Her rival's sweet orifice has been likened
to a Glade room air freshener.
The unobtrusively handy, wall-mounted spray
available in nine colors including
Mouth Watering Red, Tunnel Black
and Particularly Pink. Now, how to
make myself appear interesting without
exposing surgically enhanced nostrils,
to a capably gentile mind taking
extra classes in secular nebulisum. Or until
these carpeted hotel walls transcend the grunts
of pulsating catastrophic humping, my darlings.

The Lascivious Labyrinths of Considerate Rivals

A vacation so opportunistic
there are ashtrays,
& at night the view
is practically doctored.
Your seats are safe.
The event is free
just make your way to Hell,
ask directions of the first
Satyr you meet
ignoring the stench
of porcelain &
your altruism may transcend
even antiquity.

Establishing Then Severing All Communiques

I carried a cute little birdhouse
with a retractable bobbing head
not everywhere but to dubious locals,
roadhouses mostly and seedy atmospheric dives.
No one commented on my traditional white T-shirt,
but many patrons walked up real close
adjusting their angels of observation
back and forth, up and down
until a consensus was achieved.
Pride is a dangerous word,
& being kicked to death by a stranger
fantasy no longer seemed so absurd.

The Posthumous Wretch

Sky diving in Maku-Maku
is not conducive to longevity.
The morning mist had not yet cleared
as I mistook a crater for a field.
The locals prayed over me
encouraging my burdens to leave.
Most did conveniently, except
a stubborn glint of rectitude.
No matter how they flailed
one burning eye remained.
Ever enterprising, they stuck me on a pole
and placed us in a crop of Maku Gold
where without too much involuntary waving
I discourage the attentions of exotic crows.

The Panic Part of the Procedure

The sound of bone on bone.
Either you were assaulted
or just laconic, predisposed
to invoking inflammatory accusations.
A scratch, a short cut.
The damp hue of conjecture
can be slimy even slithery.
Tiring to run so many blocks, exactly.
Next time try and make him
feel less comfortable, throw
some playing cards on
the floor near his chair
just out of reach.

A Disturbed Perspective

The non-attendee is always lionized when
a previous planned commitment wins out.
This reunion had been compensated
with upside down M's
ashtrays and the like.
The drive here was tense.
Traffic resembled a Thomas Aquinas armada
seeking the Catholic soul of my cock.
We parked on a side street
& entered through the garden.
I mistook several women for their mothers
but before the interjection may have stopped.
The Punch's tepid taste best avoided
like epistolary references to sweet snatch.
I sat on a divan
with a column-shaped person
pestering her with questions
about this & that.

Red is the Color of My True Love's Horse

Animals have accents too.
Squirrel's provincial vowels are
complicit in their transient confinement.
Why do we allow this to occur?
I can't breakfast in peace
without overhearing tree slang
littered with caustic purrs.
The branches shake
adding to the sky's inconsistent view.
Picnic table and strawberry
plant ravished, juices strewn.
My dogs are less than useless,
preoccupied with vernaculars,
they lack the patience of nouns.

The Calming Disorder of Irrational Tendencies

Isolation
has that telling that
never begins.
Reaching the weekend house
would require similar restraint.
Little piles of rocks
benches of contemplation
nonsense dragonflies.
A dirt road when
it departed gradually,
then another rock trail
zigzagging
crazed.

The Conceptual, It's an Experience

A technician or gaffer
independent of the special effects person,
placed the clear glass table down
directly over the cameraman
who lay on his back.
The youngish model squatted on the table
and shat succinctly in good order,
two formidable turds.
This particular Angel Of Defecation
was inspired by the Franco Canarvo
school of cinema, northeast.
Essential attributions & short listed theories
remain in a shoe box with no lid.

Straight Swap

In a dusty vault, accessible
after climbing over four walls
and negotiating with a strung-out locksmith
until the formidable door stays ajar
and the locksmith leaves
seeking out his sturdies.
Perishables, blanketed drum kits
high hats mostly. A procession, nothing mystical.
Same as last words. Something
is groaning beneath a large stone floor slab
enabling us like a absolutionist's vagina,
better look as if we belong.

Gratification in the Archipelago

The recluse reluctantly consented to an interview.
Yes, the giant lizards were a problem.
They were becoming more brazen
sometimes commandeering
his entire wraparound porch.
No fans of the erudite
nor confident spellers,
they were authoritative coagulators
and would rise in unison
to the opening riff,
but not otherwise
very superstitious.

A Contract Existing to Encourage the Comparison of the Imparticular

When there is no one about,
we laborers take our lunch
on the north side of the grounds,
within the circular oak tree bench.
From here we can observe every possible approach,
even the top of a trail
leading down to the sea caves.
I often dine on gammon and local bread,
drink spring water from a metal cup.
My companions are forthcoming regarding
their wives's sleeping habits,
and demands made on all the sexes.
I usually wander off to the garden maze
where I lose myself despite familiarity.
In the very center I eventually sit
comfortably, until the afternoon resumes.
Voices climb above the hedge and birds fly off
with the indelible confidence of acclimation.

Oh's Arm Wrestling Emporium

I met the critic at four PM,
a quiet time between sets.
He was instructed, advised
to wear a muscle shirt.
He was easy to spot:
arms like tendrils,
effete and horn-rimmed.
We proceeded to the center table.
After some yoga stretching
and deep breathing he was ready.
Starting lights red to green
indicated it was time to begin.
He dislocated my wrist
within the first few seconds.
OH searched for the appropriate
toothpick umbrella,
found one with tiny cumulus clouds
and a bucolic river.

Impreciseness and Recessive Pronunciations

I am crawling to The Nebula,
taxis being in short supply.
The pavement is not accommodating.
Sellers of wares provide no comfort
seize a posture of entitlement,
hands on horticulturist defined hips.
The evening employs a charismatic hue
as I cross against the traffic.
I should have trained less for this,
rode my bike exclusively over smaller mountains
or simply grasped my ankles and rolled
into The Red Lion like pragmatists do.

Micro-Managing by Jiminy

The Pillocks have allowed
young Billy to
move back in again,
his ex a formidable ally
heiress enough for lust.
Unfortunately his portable sinner
is not that well endowed.
He has been reduced even yet
to a balm of rescission.
The blood doesn't lie still
tries, or is sincerely inspired
to breach voluptuousness
ponderously.

Relaxation in its Ethereal Aesthetic

Leaving town prematurely
I can't help but notice the innocent symmetry
of the almost straight track,
and the poofters, loitering
behind the unused coal sheds.
There is not enough time to act
until passengers overdressed
in too many layers excuse
themselves for damp soliloquy
and dreams just as effortlessly.

Mentors of the Impervious

An old trail opposed
to change.
A gate with the top slat
for comments, "I was just here" etc.
I must have missed you
because the day hadn't.
Consequently, there is misery in
your circle dotted I's.
Who takes the time
to cauterize the wood
and burn the careless pistols?
Ah sure, it's only testosterone
but it's fading just the same.

Resisting Probability

Squandered, fairly innocent
chimes hanging from a tree.
This place has suddenly become quietly profound.
Formally just the jingle of tact,
none of which was particularly happening.
Now an unthematic sound
abides inclusively.
The chimes allow someone's prayers
to catch a wind and wave phonetically.

A Landscape's Long Memory

There is no better place.
Don't succumb to hysteria
if no carpeting can last here,
or the stairs are washed away by wind.
Rope ladders still only interrogate the willing.
Every so often a straggler fantasizes
& the rainbow shits.

Malapropisms of the Mezzanine

The man was drawing
on the Apologist's Cafe Menu
a likeness for unreasonableness.
Just the basics, perishables
and an order of fries.
It was a little too early for sleeplessness,
although most people still identify mornings
later in the day.
Communication and all else between these,
can have a tendency to become personal
and anonymously esoteric.

Colin James was born in the north of England near Chester. He spent most of his youth in Massachusetts before moving back to England and working as a Postman for The Royal Mail, then as a Trackman for British Rail. He met his American wife, Jane, in Chester and they currently reside in Western Massachusetts. He is a great admirer of the Scottish landscape painter, John Mackenzie.

Photo by Liam James

www.ingramcontent.com/pod-product-compliance
Lightning Source LLC
Chambersburg PA
CBHW051702040426
42446CB00009B/1264